Useful Shrapnel
(a poem in fragments)

by

John Findura

Finishing Line Press
Georgetown, Kentucky

Useful Shrapnel
(a poem in fragments)

Copyright © 2022 by John Findura
ISBN 978-1-64662-975-6 First Edition
All rights reserved under International and Pan-American Copyright Conventions. No part of this book may be reproduced in any manner whatsoever without written permission from the publisher, except in the case of brief quotations embodied in critical articles and reviews.

ACKNOWLEDGMENTS

Some of these pieces were first lodged in *Alice Blue Review, elimae, Ghostwriters of Delphi, Sawbuck,* and *Sixth Finch*

Many, many thanks to Timothy Liu, David Shapiro, David Lehman, Elaine Equi, Mark Bibbins, Prageeta Sharma, Robert Polito, Laurie Sheck, Billy Collins, Tom Sleigh, Brian Russell, Brian Cordell, Anna & O.J. Guzon, and everyone at the Bread Loaf Writers' Conference and the Key West Literary Seminar.

A very special "Thank You!" to Noelle Kocot and Joseph Lease.

And finally, a much earned thanks to my family, my parents, and Lori, Hailey, and Chloe.

Publisher: Leah Huete de Maines
Editor: Christen Kincaid
Cover Art: John Findura
Author Photo: John Findura
Cover Design: Elizabeth Maines McCleavy

Order online: www.finishinglinepress.com
also available on amazon.com

Author inquiries and mail orders:
Finishing Line Press
PO Box 1626
Georgetown, Kentucky 40324
USA

*This is dedicated to
everyone who has had to pick the pieces back up.*

"I shall be accused of having assembled
lies, yarns, hoaxes, and superstitions.
To some degree I think so myself."
—Charles Fort, *Lo!*

This is what you do:

You make me at a loss for words
and this scares me because

Some of my best friends are words

Sometimes all I have are words and I use them
like small scalpels or baseball bats and slice things clean

Sometimes, Mercedes, for you I use them as something else
entirely

There are pieces flying
through the air—a fog
of debris caused by a
rupturing that I don't
understand—these small
fragments moving
exponentially faster for
reasons that are unclear
They leave ragged holes
in the shape of letters

Something has lodged
in my eye, deep and fractured,
driving me to focus and all I see
are letters and sometimes
they spell out words and
sometimes they spell out
my future and sometimes
I force the words to tell
me something I want to
hear—I want to hear very
important things at all times

The pond in the backyard has no water

Inside the voices grow older because all
voices grow older
and I listen to fairy tales in a foreign language

You will sing, now   for all of us

The heart is a burden and pushes down on everything
We'll spend our money inside under the vaulted ceilings
of strange hotel lobbies

I don't remember any of your names except for Mercedes

I will refer to you by blinking three times

I will squeeze my hand until my knuckles crack
I will not click my teeth, although I will want to

Now that I am blown apart I spend more time on the untanned
parts of your body
In every way these are the most important

I change my shirt multiple times leaving
sweat-stained collars in each—

I begin to realize that the line where fictions begin emanates from
me like an aura

She shakes a finger covertly   I, swear you're—

When they ask who's in charge
point to your shoes

and when they ask what that means

just smile and whisper nothing

Everyone was oh so weak—

And yet they still complained to you, Mercedes,
even though you have come home

I assumed you had dark hair
I am very good at assuming

Of course I was correct

I collect the broken
things and I reform
them into what I think
they should look like
which is often words
that amuse only me

We never did more than we did

That is a simple, verifiable fact

Even your fingers know that
but mine forget so easily and often

One of us should have made an/the attempt

Mercedes, why did you get married and never tell me?
Why are there children in all the photos of you?

Don't say because you didn't know me yet—
that is the oldest excuse

Yes, that was the recurring nightmare that washed over me

The house is older than I thought
It is all wood and has lasted

There are no neighbors. There are white lace curtains

Draw a map of the rooms
So we'll know where to hide

This has all gone
over my head
very rapidly—I can
smell the propellant
in the air and yet
I maintain that this
is the best of all
possible worlds
because I believe
in some sort of
philosophy or magic

You are that forbidden apple walking down a hallway
and everyone is hungry. Are you offended? I am

Every time I listen to Tom Waits I want to taste you

You made up lyrics
No, I made up lyrics you made up a melody

The lyrics were not there before we arrived
so one of us made them up and you sang them

I ran my fingers over the six strings
you sang the lyrics   I wrote the song

There are contrails
following me as if
they are targeting
me and my thoughts
they plow through
the word balloons
I imagine over my
head every time I
have a good thought
and it bothers me
most that I find this
so utterly reassuring

Ah, my legs had disappeared
into a pack of squirrels
and by that I mean
something incomprehensible

Of course I will not
be able to stand
and there aren't really any squirrels

I sent you a message that I mean—
Please don't break my windowpane

Although that was not the message
it comes damn close—just replace
the words with other words

No, I don't know which

I learned to communicate over years
so I could eventually speak in codes.

You never learned the code. I pretend
you understand it and speak to an assortment of liars

Mercedes, do you know the code?

I don't think anyone knows the code so
there are messages bouncing around
that are undecipherable

These are like seeds falling on concrete
but invisible   and silent

This is not ridiculous
If I knew other words
I would use them to crack open things

I'm just not sure what things

Do you believe in invisibility?
Do you see me tapping my fingers?

I'm not even sure what I put in my body
and what was there before

I forget how I feel now compared to then

You have many
shapes in which
you display not
only yourself but
also your thoughts
and your likes,
dislikes, combinations
of both and the
colors of dresses
you plan on buying
for that dinner to
which I may or may
not have been invited

What has fallen on you, Mercedes?

Years and years, responsibility and bad tips
You are only responsible for one of them

Do you remember when your
messages stopped, Mercedes?

(I forget who I am talking to)
I'm sure you had your reasons

I'm sure you had a lot of things

This dress you might be
wearing may be back-less
you might be unsure
how to describe what
you will be wearing to me
while I have many
descriptions I could
give such a garment

The trucks were parked in geometric patterns
Everyone assumed it was high science

It was providence

Everyone went to the diner drunk, anyway

Did you hear me speak to Mercedes?
Once she moved faster than the speed of light
But that is impossible
      So now you understand

One of us was very wrong
and then she brought me coffee

I asked if I paid her and then she
had three children and a house with
a big backyard, that quickly—

I slept under the sink once

Everyone washed their hands
and no one woke me

I am tired of
not being a bird
of being a lowly
land animal
straining my eyes
while looking up
and knowing I
will never get a
chance to taste
the clouds I long
to taste and believe
they have a taste

I become easily
distracted by the
squirrels running
along the power
lines with such
grace and honesty
that I never picture
them slipping and
falling to the black
top warm with car
tires and exhaust
where I, without
fail, find them

You asked for stories that I knew from my youth
I said they were not stories

You said to tell them anyway, that I am good at lying

Sound travels very
fast and I know this
because I can see it
moving this way
at unsafe speeds and
when I say *I can
see it* what I mean
is that I don't hear it
but I am somehow
still perceiving its
trippingly limber
limbs glide across
whatever landscape
has been painted
quickly between us

When I watched
the explosion I did
not think so many
fragments would
come my way
buzz my cheeks
this smooth cut
my tongue any
deeper than it is
but I know I can
be wrong about
many things and
look what we have
found here: many
peculiar things

One was the truth, one was a story
Not the one you think
Possibly not the one I think

How many did I tell?

Mercedes, just lie down with me for a moment
We don't have to touch

but I need to think

and you help me think

I will not tap my fingers three times,
and I will not tell you

Although I will want to

John Findura is the author of the poetry collection *Submerged* (Five Oaks Press, 2017). He holds an MFA in Poetry from The New School, an M.Ed in Professional Counseling from William Paterson University, and an Ed.D in Educational Technology Leadership from New Jersey City University. His poetry and criticism appear in numerous journals including *Verse; Fourteen Hills; Copper Nickel; Pleiades; Forklift, Ohio; Sixth Finch; Prelude;* and *Rain Taxi*. He has worked as a Middle School and High School English teacher, an adolescent psychotherapist, and has taught everything from Composition & Literature to Intercultural Communications to Technical Writing at various colleges. Since 2009 he has been the Writing Center Supervisor at Bergen Community College's national award-winning Cerullo Learning Assistance Center. A guest blogger for *The Best American Poetry*, he lives in Northern New Jersey with his wife and two daughters.

www.ingramcontent.com/pod-product-compliance
Lightning Source LLC
LaVergne TN
LVHW041518070426
835507LV00012B/1653